Great Book of
EGG DECORATING

To Luciana, Federico, Luisa, and Francesca

WARM THANKS TO:

Gigi Longo, Leone Greco, and Anna Varetto for their understanding, assistance,
and collaboration and for having believed in our work.
Our grandfathers and children for their enthusiasm and patience.

A particularly warm thanks to:
DOBA, Centro Culturale Ceco, Turin;
and to FERRUA, Turin.

Editor: Cristina Sperandeo
Photography: Alberto Bertoldi and Mario Matteucci
Graphic design and layout: Paola Maserra and Amelia Verga
Translation: Chiara Tarsia

Library of Congress Cataloging-in-Publication Data Available

1   3   5   7   9   10   8   6   4   2

First paperback edition published in 2000 by
Sterling Publishing Company, Inc.
387 Park Avenue South, New York, N.Y. 10016
Originally published in Italy and © 1998 by R.C.S. Libri
& Grandi Opere S.p.A., Milan, under the title *Uovo Decorate*
English translation © 1999 by Sterling Publishing Company
Distributed in Canada by Sterling Publishing
c/o Canadian Manda Group, One Atlantic Avenue, Suite 105
Toronto, Ontario, Canada M6K 3E7
Distributed in Great Britain and Europe by Cassell PLC
Wellington House, 125 Strand, London WC2R 0BB, England
Distributed in Australia by Capricorn Link (Australia) Pty Ltd.
P.O. Box 6651, Baulkham Hills, Business Centre, NSW 2153, Australia

Printed in China

Sterling ISBN 0-8069-5911-8 Trade
0-8069-5912-6 Paper

Great Book of EGG DECORATING

Grazia Buttafuoco
& Dede Varetto

Sterling Publishing Co., Inc.
New York

CONTENTS

WAX EMBOSSING ON NATURAL SHELLS 14

WAX EMBOSSING ON COLORED SHELLS 36

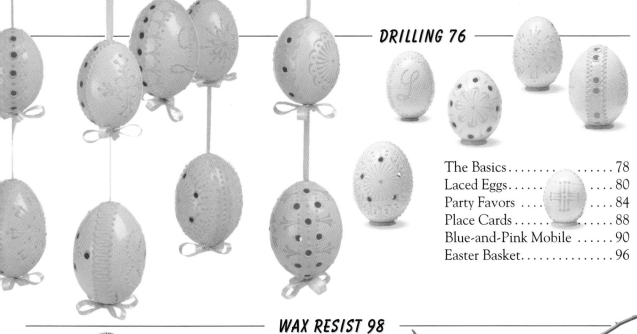

DRILLING 76

WAX RESIST 98

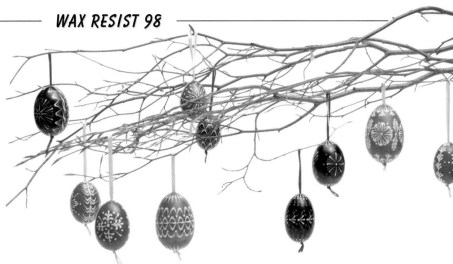

DECOUPAGE 110

INTRODUCTION

We first saw decorated eggs while traveling in Czechoslovakia. Always on the lookout for gifts that are not only beautiful but also unusual, we are never particularly drawn to traditional souvenir shops. One day, though, we found a tiny shop in Prague that featured decorated eggs. Basket after basket was filled to the brim with red, black, and yellow painted eggs. Our intention was to buy lots of these pretty eggs for our families and friends back home as souvenirs of our trip, but we never did give any away and instead wound up keeping all of the eggs for ourselves. They are now on display in our homes, nestled safely inside crystal goblets.

An art teacher in Prague taught us the local egg decorating techniques, which we tried on chicken, goose, and duck eggs. As we experimented, we developed our own designs that had a unique blend of Slavic tradition and Italian creativity, and we decided to write this book so that we could share our enthusiasm and techniques with others.

The more we traveled, the more we discovered just how widespread a tradition decorating eggs is. But what are its histori-

cal roots?

The egg has always been considered a symbol of life. According to the ancient Egyptians, the egg combines the four elements of the universe: air, water, earth, and fire. Jews used to offer an egg as a gift to friends on the first day of the new year or on birthdays. With the advent of springtime, people in the Slavic regions decorated eggs (a symbol of fertility and love) to give as presents or for decorating their homes. Medieval farmers placed an egg at each end of a plowed furrow to mark and bless the open and close of each growing season. Soothsayers used eggs to predict the future. According to one ancient Greek legend, Mary Magdalene upon her arrival in Rome appeared before the Emperor Tiberius with a red egg, supposedly foretelling the resurrection of Christ. Although many legends about the egg have come and gone, the custom of exchanging eggs at Easter still endures. In many countries it is still common practice to decorate eggs with traditional motifs and techniques that can turn an ordinary eggshell into an artistic collectible.

The techniques in this book are those most frequently seen and treasured the world over. Enjoy!

THE EGGS

Artificial eggs can be made of wood, porcelain, plastic, or polystyrene. We experimented extensively on artificial eggs before graduating to real eggs, with which we think we created even more beautiful results.

The biggest challenge presented by a real egg is the fragility of its shell, although it is perhaps just that fragility that fascinates us. Eggs of all types of birds can be decorated using the techniques in this book. The most common types of eggs are listed below.

EGG GUIDE

OSTRICH EGGS

Ostrich eggs are elegant with their finely pitted ivory-colored shells. They seem gigantic when compared to chicken eggs. In fact, the content of one ostrich egg is equivalent to that of about twenty chicken eggs! To find ostrich eggs, you might try specialty shops or farms. Ostriches are raised in Australia, New Zealand, South Africa, Canada, and the United States, among other countries. Eggs can be purchased both full and blown; we recommend blown eggs because they generally cost less than full eggs, because the blowing has already been done for you, and because blown shells can usually be found year round. Prices can vary considerably, even for blown eggs.

GOOSE EGGS

Goose eggs are smaller than ostrich eggs and larger than chicken eggs. Goose eggs are white and usually available only during the first half of the year. Before buying goose eggs, always make sure they are not dirty to the point that their dark haloes can't be washed away. Refer to Tricks of the Trade, page 124, for tips on cleaning eggs.

Ostrich   Goose   Chicken

DUCK EGGS

Duck eggs have smooth shells that are less fragile than chicken eggs. They are white or creamy in color and are available year round. The size of duck eggs can vary. This type of egg is particularly suited for drilling.

CHICKEN EGGS

Chicken eggs come in assorted sizes, colors, and shapes. Just about everyone knows what a chicken egg looks like, but here are some tips:

- The size of an egg is not nearly as important as a pleasing shape.
- The smoother the shell, the better the decorative results.
- Eggs that have a thick shell and no cracks work best.
- The color of the shell can range from white to pink to brown, depending upon the breed and diet of the chicken.
- Leghorns are a Mediterranean breed that lay eggs with exceptionally white shells. Their eggs are difficult to find and are available only at certain times of year.

QUAIL EGGS

Quail eggs are much smaller than chicken eggs and have very fragile shells. They are speckled, come in a variety of colors, and can be displayed just as they are, without any decoration. If you prefer to leave your quail eggs natural, give them a coat of varnish to preserve them and make the shell more sturdy. Remember that it is possible to whiten eggs by washing them; refer to Tricks of the Trade, page 124. Quail eggs are available year round.

Leghorn chicken   American chicken   Duck   Dove   Quail

BLOWING EGGS

WHAT YOU'LL NEED

- Soap
- Soft brush or a sponge
- Hard pencil
- Tapestry needle
- Bowls
- Warm water
- Vinegar

Traditionally all decorated eggs were hardboiled and, therefore, did not last long. Today eggs are usually blown, which allows them to last much longer. Blowing eggs may at first seem to be a tedious and exacting process, but if you follow our instructions, you will be amazed how easy it really is.

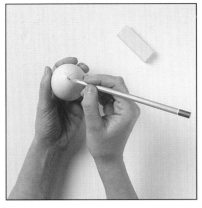

1 Wash the egg with soap and a soft brush or scouring sponge, both for cleanliness and to get rid of stains and crustiness. If any stains prove particularly difficult, follow the tips in Tricks of the Trade, page 124.

2 With a pencil, mark the two opposite ends of the egg, making sure the marks are centered.

3 Using a tapestry needle, pierce the egg at the marks, then widen the holes slightly.

4 Working over a bowl, blow firmly into one of the two holes in the egg; the white and yolk will flow out the opposite hole. If you are unable to blow the entire contents with one breath, shake the egg well and blow again.

5 You can freeze the white and yolk if you will not be using them immediately in cooking.

6 Rinse the egg well and soak it in a bowl of warm water and vinegar (8 oz. of vinegar for every 28 oz. of water) to prevent mold from developing. Allow the egg to dry thoroughly, at least 2 hours, before decorating it; wax will not adhere to a wet surface.

WAX EMBOSSING ON NATURAL SHELLS

Embossing with wax is one of the oldest Slavic egg-decorating techniques, and it has remained popular to this day. Anyone can do the embossing, even those who have little confidence in their artistic ability. There are only a few basic strokes and patterns, and they can be combined and recombined to make an endless number of different designs.

THE BASICS

- Beeswax is available in sheet and pellet form; we recommend the pellets because they are generally easier to measure out for use.
- Paraffin wax is available in candle, block, flake, and pellet form. The wax must be pure white for later dying, or you can purchase wax that is already dyed.
- Wax crayons or pastels are sold as individual sticks or in boxes of assorted colors in crafts shops and art supply stores. Dyes made especially for wax are also available.
- Small paraffin stoves are widely available in some parts of the world, but if you can't find one in your local crafts shop, you could make the one shown here out of small wooden boards; a metal bowl or spoon; a wing nut, screw, and washer; and a small bottle below the bowl containing paraffin wax and a wick.
- A pin stylus is used to paint the embossing wax onto the egg in uniform strokes and dots. To make the stylus, insert the tip of an all-steel straight pin into the end of a narrow dowel or pencil. The head of the pin is the end you will paint with, and it must be metal so that it won't melt when dipped into hot wax.
- An alternative tool for painting with wax is the kistka (not shown here; available in crafts shops), which consists of a small metal funnel attached to a stick wrapped with copper wire. The tool comes in different sizes for making different line widths. Electric kistkas are also available.

PREPARING THE WAX

Wax embossing is done with a mixture of melted and dyed paraffin wax and beeswax.

- Before beginning, prepare all the colored waxes that you intend to use; this will save time once you get down to work.
- You can use purchased precolored wax or mix your own colors using wax crayons, pastels, or dyes.
- To make dark colors of wax with crayons or pastels, add a small amount of white and then the main color. To make light colors, prepare white wax as a base, and then add just a little coloring.
- Between color changes, clean the bowl thoroughly, or use a separate bowl for each color.

  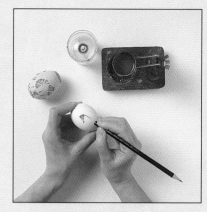

1 Place equal amounts of paraffin wax and beeswax into a bowl on the paraffin stove. If the wax is undyed, add wax crayons, pastels, or special wax dyes.

2 Turn on the stove and carefully mix the ingredients with a pin; the wax will be ready for use in a few minutes.

3 Practice embossing on a test egg first.

4 Before painting each stroke on the egg, you must dip the pin on the stylus into the bowl of melted wax, working quickly to prevent the wax from solidifying on the pin.

5 If the wax is too hot, it will begin to smoke and to slide down the eggshell; the color of the wax will darken.

6 If the wax is not hot enough, it will remain dense and not flow smoothly; the stroke will look irregular.

7 Melted wax is highly flammable, so always observe safety precautions.

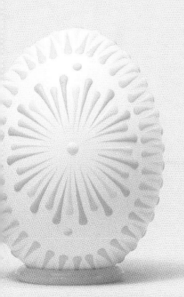  

RED ROSETTES

A wide variety of embossed designs can be painted on eggs, so let your creativity be your guide. Remember that each design can have either a horizontal or vertical orientation.

WHAT YOU'LL NEED

- White chicken or duck eggs
- Red wax
- Paraffin stove
- Pin stylus

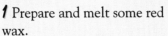
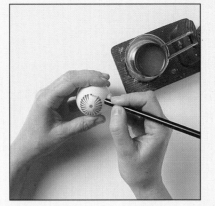
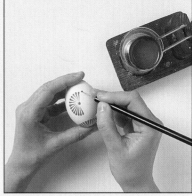

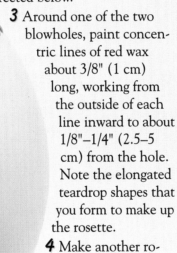

1 Prepare and melt some red wax.

2 Hold the pin stylus in your dominant hand and carefully hold the egg in the other. Dip the pin into the melted wax and start decorating the eggs as directed below.

3 Around one of the two blowholes, paint concentric lines of red wax about 3/8" (1 cm) long, working from the outside of each line inward to about 1/8"–1/4" (2.5–5 cm) from the hole. Note the elongated teardrop shapes that you form to make up the rosette.

4 Make another rosette around the second blowhole.

5 With a drop of wax, make a dot halfway between the two blowholes, and around this dot paint another rosette. On the opposite side of the egg, make another central dot and another rosette.

- Work quickly to make each dot or stroke so that the wax does not harden on the pin. If you find it difficult to make lines of the same length, keep practicing until you are satisfied with the results.

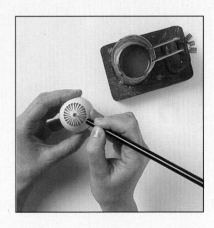

6 If you don't intend to hang the egg, you can seal one or both blowholes; sealed holes make the egg look more complete.

- Paint around the edges of each hole again and again, working inward to the center of the hole, closing it.

7 You can further embellish a rosette by painting an additional short stroke of wax between each pair of longer strokes; paint the shorter strokes from the outside inward so that all the strokes face the same direction.
- Complete the design by painting a dot just beyond the outer tip of each short stroke; make all the dots equidistant from their respective strokes.

8 You can make a variation of the rosette by painting the second (shorter) set of strokes in step 7 from the inside outward.
- Complete the design by painting a dot over the outer tip of each of the longer strokes.

- Add scallops around the rosette.
- For this design a drop of wax was painted inside each scallop.

9 You can fill the empty spaces between rosettes by making a central dot surrounded by 4–5 equidistant dots, or by making dots in any design you prefer.

BLUE ROSETTES

These pretty blue designs on an ostrich egg may
look difficult, but with a little practice
all of your eggs will be picture perfect.

HOW-TO'S

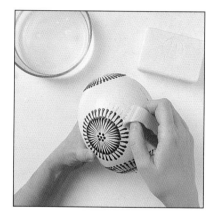

1 You can mark the design on
the egg first by using a pencil
and compass if you prefer not to
do your embossing freehand.

2 Paint the blue rosettes on the
ostrich egg in the same manner
as for the Red Rosettes, page 20.

3 Use a soft brush to get rid of
any remaining pencil marks. Do
not use an eraser, which will
smear the pencil marks and ruin
your egg.

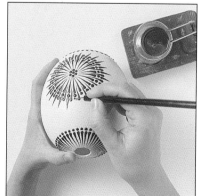

4 To make a fancier egg, you
can paint more elaborate
rosettes.

5 After the embossing is complete, wash the egg in cold
water using soap and the soft
brush to eliminate any stubborn
stains and remaining pencil
marks.

SUMMER CENTERPIECE

WHAT YOU'LL NEED

- White eggs embossed with white wax
- Floral picks
- Floral sponge
- Sharp knife, scissors
- Ceramic bowl
- Ferns, variegated ivy
- Pale pink roses, white lysanthiums, baby's breath

1 Prepare 12–15 eggs embossed with white rosettes and any other desired designs. Seal one blowhole on each egg; see step 6 on page 21.

2 Into each open blowhole, insert the unsharpened end of a floral pick.

3 Using a sharp knife, cut and shape the floral sponge, then wet the sponge and place it in the ceramic bowl.

4 Poke some fern and ivy into the sponge to cover the rim of the bowl; add some at the center of the sponge.

5 Insert roses and lysanthiums, trimming them to the desired length with scissors; fill in the spaces with baby's breath.

6 Add the eggs, poking the sharp ends of the floral picks into the sponge, beginning at the center of the arrangement and working outward.

7 You can use eggs of assorted sizes for an interesting variation.

- Remember, as you add elements to the arrangement, that it should not grow in height.

- The centerpiece will last longer if you keep the sponge moist and spray the flowers and leaves daily with water; the water will not harm the eggs.

MULTICOLORED EGGS

These sophisticated designs display beautiful color effects.

1 Starting at one of the blow-holes, use a pencil to mark a grid of diamonds all over a brown egg.
- Note that the diamonds will be larger at the center of the egg than at the ends.

2 Prepare and melt some brown wax.
3 Emboss the grid lines with brown wax, making each leg of each diamond a separate stroke.

4 Prepare and heat some white wax, then use it to draw a fleur-de-lis inside every diamond; make the long center stroke first and then the two shorter outer strokes. All of the flowers should face the same direction.
- Near the ends of the egg, where the diamonds are smaller, you may prefer to draw only the two shorter strokes of the fleur-de-lis.
- You can use a variety of colors for the flowers as long as the overall effect is pleasing.

WHAT YOU'LL NEED

- Brown chicken egg
- Hard pencil
- Brown and white waxes
- Paraffin stove
- Pin stylus

AUTUMN CENTERPIECE

A typical autumn arrangement, this centerpiece would be
a welcome seasonal decoration in any decor.

WHAT YOU'LL NEED

- Multicolored embossed eggs
- Floral picks
- Sharp knife, scissors
- Floral sponge
- Deep copper tray
- Oak or similar leaves and branches
- Wire
- Fresh or dried gourds,
pomegranates, corn, poppy pods,
berries, saffron, chestnuts, acorns

1 Using a sharp knife, cut and shape a floral sponge to fit into a copper tray firmly; add a second smaller layer of sponge at the center of the tray.

2 Poke the oak leaves into the sponge to cover the rim of the bowl.

3 Add a few oak branches, about 6"–8" (15–20 cm) high, at the center back of the tray.

4 Wire the gourds and pomegranates, then arrange them around the small upper sponge at the center of the tray.

5 Wire the corn and insert it in front of the oak branches.

6 Add the poppy pods, trimming them to the desired length with scissors.

7 Insert the unsharpened end of a floral pick into the open blowhole of each prepared egg.

8 Poke the eggs and berries into the top of the small upper sponge.

9 Fill the sparse areas with saffron, chestnuts, and acorns.

WAX EMBOSSING ON COLORED SHELLS

Glossy, satiny, or opaque . . . yellow, red, or black . . .
colored eggs have a charm all their own, which is enhanced
by elegant wax embossing.

THE BASICS

- Wax embossing can also be done on dyed and painted eggs.
- Until recently only natural colors were used for eggs. To make a purple-red color, for instance, the liquid from cooking red onions was used. To make eggs yellow, they were dipped into water and saffron. To make eggs green, they were dipped into the liquid from crushed unripened wheat.
- Today we use inks, dyes, paints, varnishes, and other synthetic colorings on eggs. There are types of colorings available for all types of uses.
- Always wear rubber gloves when coloring eggs to protect your hands from dyes and to prevent any possible allergic reaction. Remember to wear an apron or old clothes because most dyes and inks are indelible.

INKS

- Black India ink covers exceptionally well; colored India inks give a transparent effect that is very attractive. Bronze and gold are other colors you might consider using.
- Remember that not all types of ink adhere well to eggshells, so be sure to try your inks on a test egg.
- Give the egg two thin coats of ink instead of one thick one, using soft, medium-size paintbrushes.

DYES

- The pigments used to dye fabrics are made from powders melted in hot water. The same dyes can be used to color eggs.
- The intensity of the color depends on many factors, including the temperature and length of the dip.

- Never use any fixative that may come in the dye package.

PAINTS

- Water-based acrylic paints are opaque and cover well. They are quick to dry.
- Acrylics come in a wide range of colors, including pearls and metallics.
- Give the egg 2 thin coats of paint instead of one thick one, using soft, medium-size paintbrushes.

VARNISHES

- Varnish, shellac, and clear acrylic spray are all suitable finishes for decorated eggs.
- A clear, glossy finish will seal the egg and enhance the look of all colors from light to dark.
- Apply thin coats of varnish and allow adequate drying time between coats.

RED EGGS

These bright and colorful eggs are perfect to give as a gift
or to decorate your home for a festive occasion.

WHAT YOU'LL NEED

- Chicken eggs
- Red varnish
- Paintbrush
- Wooden skewer
- White wax
- Paraffin stove
- Pin stylus

1 Paint the egg with red varnish, using a soft paintbrush. To make it easier you can thread a wooden skewer through the egg to support it while you apply varnish with long brush strokes.
- Give the egg 2–3 coats, allowing the varnish to dry.

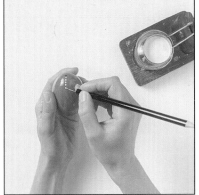

2 Heat some white wax and make a straight row of closely spaced white wax dots between blowholes; continue along the opposite side of the egg, dividing it into halves.

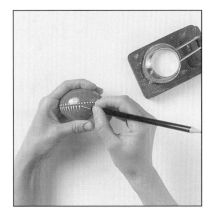

3 Hold the egg horizontally and make a row of strokes extending downward below each dot; space them a small distance away from the dots so that the dots and strokes are equidistant. Make another row of strokes extending upward above each dot.

4 Make another row of strokes above and below the dotted lines, but this time draw them from the outside inward.
- Make all of the lines equidistant with their ends in a straight line.

5 You can decorate the center of each half of the egg with an 8-pointed star if you like. Make the strokes from the center outward.

6 Add a dot between each pair of star points.
- You can add other designs as desired, but bear in mind that the use of the pin head as a stylus will limit your choices.

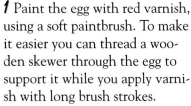

PINK WREATH

An egg wreath would be pretty at Easter, but it can also be used to celebrate the birth of a newborn or any special birthday.

WHAT YOU'LL NEED

- 7 chicken eggs
- Pink varnish
- Paintbrush
- Wooden skewers
- Pink and white waxes
- Paraffin stove
- Pin stylus
- Wire, curtain ring
- Pink or white floral tape
- White mesh ribbon
- Needle, white thread, scissors

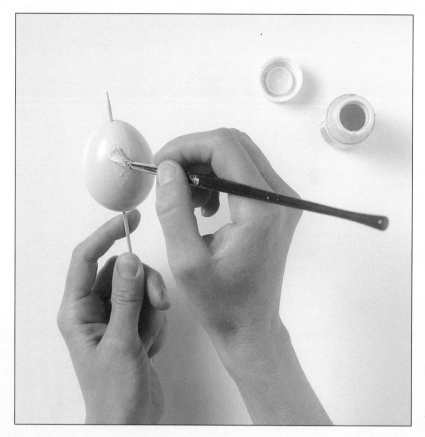

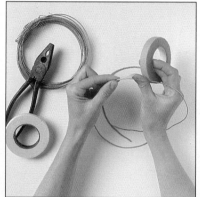

1 Paint the eggs with pink varnish, using a soft paintbrush. - Give each egg 2–3 coats, allowing the varnish to dry thoroughly after each coat.

2 Decorate the eggs as you prefer, using the pink and white waxes. You can decorate each egg with either one or both colors of wax.

3 Cut a piece of wire about 24" (60 cm) long. Cover it with floral tape.

4 Carefully thread the wire through the eggs and twist the ends together, forming a wreath.
5 Make 6 identical bows from the mesh ribbon (or add a second ribbon and tie both ribbons together into less transparent bows).

6 Use needle and thread to secure the bows between pairs of eggs.
7 Add a large mesh bow at the bottom of the wreath, or double the white mesh ribbon with a pink satin one and tie them together in a decorative bow.
8 Sew the curtain ring to the back of the wreath for a hanger.

LIGHT BLUE WREATH

WHAT YOU'LL NEED

- 10 chicken, dove, and quail eggs
- Light blue and white varnishes
- Paintbrushes
- Wooden skewers
- Light blue and white waxes
- Paraffin stove
- Pin stylus
- Cardboard, compass
- Scissors, utility knife
- Polyester batting
- Fabric glue
- Light blue and white tulle
- Light blue and white organdy ribbons
- Light blue and white checked satin ribbons
- Sewing needle, light blue thread
- Curtain rings
- Straight pins, measuring tape

1 Color 5 eggs with light blue varnish and 5 with white varnish.

2 Prepare the light blue and white waxes. Emboss some eggs with light blue wax, others with white wax, and some using both colors.

- Remember that there is no need to decorate parts of an egg that will not be visible on the finished project.

3 Seal the blowholes; see step 6 on page 21.

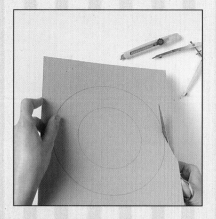

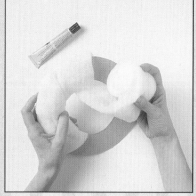

4 Prepare the base of the wreath. On a piece of cardboard, draw 2 concentric circles, one with a 4" (10 cm) radius and the other with a 2" (5 cm) radius.
- Cut out the wreath shape from the cardboard.

5 Cut long strips 3" (8 cm) wide from the polyester batting. Wind the batting around the cardboard wreath, securing it with a drop of glue.
6 Cover the padded wreath with blue tulle; glue or stitch in place.

7 Sew a curtain ring to the back of the wreath for a hanger, if you wish.

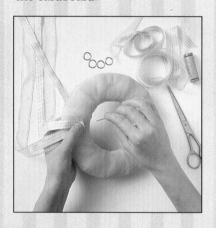

8 Make assorted single and double bows from the satin and organdy ribbons.

9 Position the bows on the wreath as desired, using straight pins.
- Sew on the bows with needle and thread.

10 Glue the eggs to the wreath between the bows, arranging them as desired.
11 Cut about 31" (80 cm) of satin and organdy ribbon. Overlap, fold, and sew them to the wreath.

NAVY-AND-WHITE MOBILE

A unique mobile painted in elegant navy blue and white. How pretty!

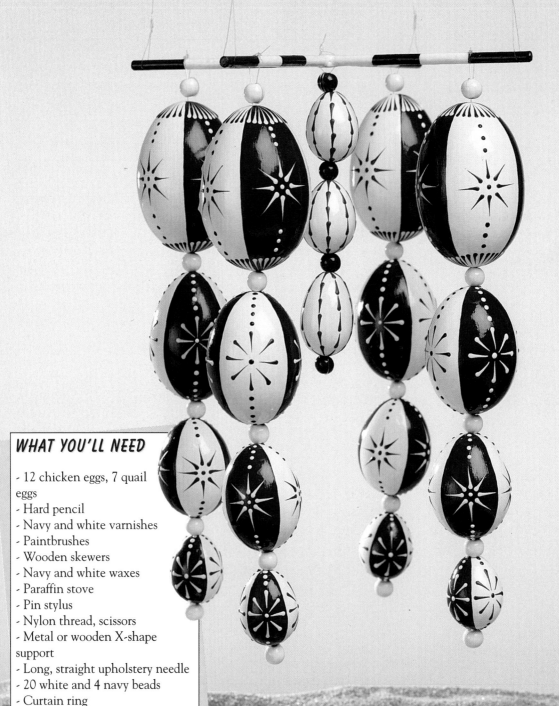

WHAT YOU'LL NEED

- 12 chicken eggs, 7 quail eggs
- Hard pencil
- Navy and white varnishes
- Paintbrushes
- Wooden skewers
- Navy and white waxes
- Paraffin stove
- Pin stylus
- Nylon thread, scissors
- Metal or wooden X-shape support
- Long, straight upholstery needle
- 20 white and 4 navy beads
- Curtain ring

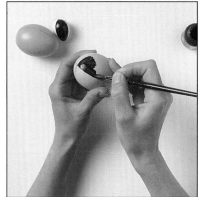

1 Set aside 3 quail eggs for the short center strand. Divide each of the remaining eggs into 4 equal top-to-bottom segments; they will be used to make the longer outer strands.

2 Cover 2 opposite segments of each egg with navy varnish, using the pencil marks as guides.
- Allow the eggs to dry, following the manufacturer's directions.

3 Paint the unvarnished segments on each egg with white varnish.
- Apply several coats of white varnish, allowing adequate drying time after each coat.

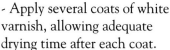

4 Paint the remaining 3 quail eggs with white varnish.
- Apply several coats of varnish to create adequate coverage and to strengthen the shell.

5 Draw your patterns on a sheet of paper before beginning to emboss the eggs with wax.
6 On each segment of each navy-and-white egg, make an 8-point star or rosette, alternating the designs.
7 Join the rosettes and stars to their respective blowholes with two series of dots, as shown.

8 Divide each egg into 8 equal top-to-bottom segments, then draw a series of strokes along each marked line with navy wax.

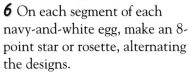

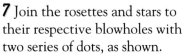

9 Cut the nylon thread into 5 equal lengths, about 24" (60 cm) each.

10 Use the upholstery needle to alternately thread white beads and eggs. Start with a bead to which you have anchored the wire, and then continue adding an egg and another bead; add eggs from the smallest to the largest and end with a bead at the top.

11 Complete 4 strands as directed in step 10; make a loop at the top of each strand.

12 Assemble the center strand, alternating navy beads with the 3 white quail eggs.

13 Paint the X-shape support with navy and white varnish. You can make 2 arms navy and 2 white or alternate colors on each arm.

14 Cut 2 equal lengths of nylon thread and insert them through the curtain ring.

15 Arrange on the X-shape support the long outer strands of eggs and the short center strand.

We suggest that you use eggs of assorted sizes for this mobile. We used (from top to bottom on each long strand) a double-yolk chicken egg, a Leghorn chicken egg, an American chicken egg, and a quail egg. Quail eggs were also used for the shorter strand.

NOTE CARDS

Are you pleased with the decorated eggs you have made so far?
Take pictures of the ones you like best and use them to make personalized
note cards for sending to friends and relatives.

WHAT YOU'LL NEED

- Photographs of decorated eggs
- Note cards with photo frame covers
- Drafting T- or L-square
- Clear tape

- Using the carpenter's T- or L-square, center each egg photograph behind a note-card frame; stick in place with clear tape.
- You can decorate the frames if you wish, painting them solid colors or using individual motifs.

AUTUMN DOOR ORNAMENT

This attractive composition was inspired by the warm colors of autumn.
Let it brighten up your door and warmly welcome your guests.

WHAT YOU'LL NEED

- 6–8 chicken and quail eggs
- Olive-green varnish
- Paintbrush, toothpick
- Wooden skewers
- White wax
- Paraffin stove
- Pin stylus
- Nylon thread, scissors
- Wire
- Curtain ring
- 2 dried ears of corn with leaves
- Chinese lanterns on branches
- Brown mesh ribbon

1 Paint the eggs with olive-green varnish. Give each egg several coats, allowing the varnish to dry thoroughly after each coat.

2 Emboss the ends of each egg with white wax.

3 Emboss the sides of the eggs, making different designs on each egg.

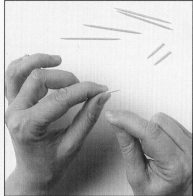

4 Seal the blowhole at the base of each egg; see step 6 on page 21.

5 Cut a toothpick to about 3/4" (2 cm) long. Thread some nylon thread around its center.

6 Insert the toothpick into the remaining blowhole so that it will remain fixed inside the egg.

7 Spread the leaves of the corn, arranging them attractively.

8 Use a piece of wire to tie the leaves of both ears of corn together.

9 Thread the curtain ring through the wire on the back of the corn; it will be the hanger.

10 Wire some Chinese lanterns to the corn.

11 Test-fit the eggs and adjust the length of the nylon threads.

12 Tie the eggs carefully to the corn.

13 Complete the decoration by adding a large ribbon bow.

CHRISTMAS DOOR ORNAMENT

WHAT YOU'LL NEED

- Evergreen tree branch
- 7–8 assorted chicken eggs
- Paintbrushes
- Red varnish, gold paint
- #3 hard pencil
- Wooden skewers
- Red and gold waxes
- Paraffin stove
- Pin stylus
- Red satin ribbon 1/2" (1.5 cm) wide
- Nylon thread, scissors
- Toothpicks
- Yellow cord
- Gold lamé ribbon 2 1/2" (6.5 cm) wide
- Sewing needle, red thread
- Gold-striped organdy ribbon

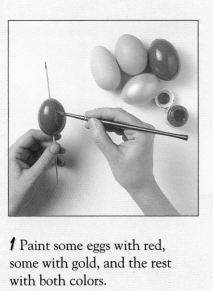

- Use skewers as supports during painting to avoid smearing the colors.

1 Paint some eggs with red, some with gold, and the rest with both colors.

- You can also divide the egg into 4 equal top-to-bottom segments with a pencil and then paint the segments alternately red and gold.

2 Prepare the red and gold waxes. Emboss the gold eggs with red wax and the red eggs with gold wax.

3 Make simple embossed scallops along the dividing lines between the red and gold in order to help hide them.

4 Seal the blowholes with either red or gold wax; see step 6 on page 21.

5 Cut a piece of nylon thread about 10" (25 cm) long, twist it around a piece of toothpick 3/4"–1" (2–3 cm) long, and fasten it.

6 Insert the toothpick completely into the egg. Prepare one toothpick for each egg.

7 Prepare one cord-and-red-ribbon bow for each egg.

8 Thread the nylon cord that extends from the toothpick in each egg through a needle, and sew it to the center of a cord-and-ribbon bow.

9 Arrange the ribbon on top of the egg and secure it with nylon thread.

10 Form a loop at the free end of the nylon thread.
11 Use the loop to hang the egg on the branch.

12 Use the gold lamé ribbon to make a large decorative single or double bow.

13 Fasten the gold bow to the branch.

WINDOW ORNAMENTS

Although they are most commonly seen at Easter, decorated eggs can
be displayed at any time of year. For Christmas and New Year's, for instance,
you could decorate your windows using eggs and ribbons in seasonal colors
such as red, green, gold, and silver.

WHAT YOU'LL NEED

- Chicken eggs
- Red and black varnishes
- Wooden skewers, paintbrush
- White wax
- Paraffin stove
- Pin stylus
- Silver metallic cord
- Silver ribbon 3/8" (1 cm) wide
- Silver or gray thread
- Sewing needle, scissors
- Long, straight upholstery needle
- Thumbtacks or push pins

1 Paint some eggs with red varnish and others with black.

2 Emboss the eggs with white wax. You can paint the same design on every egg or make them all different.

3 Use the silver ribbon to prepare one 4-loop bow for each egg.

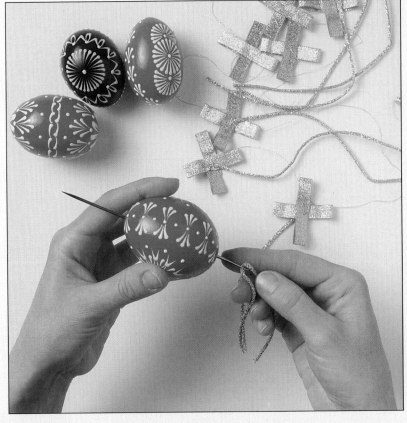

4 Cut the silver cord into various lengths and sew one to each bow.

You can replace the silver cords and ribbons with red and black trims. You can also eliminate the cords and ribbons, then display the eggs all in a row.

5 Thread the free end of the silver cord through the eye of the needle and insert the needle through the egg's blowholes.
6 On the window frame make a mark where you want to hang each egg. Attach the silver cord with thumbtacks or push pins. Hide the tacks by covering them with silver bows.

GOLD CHRISTMAS ORNAMENTS

WHAT YOU'LL NEED

- 15–18 quail eggs
- Gold paint
- Wooden skewers
- Paraffin stove
- Pin stylus
- Fabric glue
- Gold-edged white satin ribbon
1/4" (6 mm) wide
- Scissors, measuring tape,
paintbrush
- Artificial evergreen tree about
12" (30 cm) high

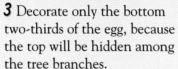

1 Paint the quail eggs gold. Give each egg several coats to cover well.

2 Prepare white wax and use it to emboss the eggs.

3 Decorate only the bottom two-thirds of the egg, because the top will be hidden among the tree branches.

4 Seal the blowholes; see step 6 on page 21.

5 Working from the bottom of the tree upward, carefully arrange and glue the eggs on it.

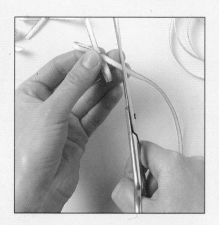

6 Use the ribbon to prepare 20–30 single or double bows.

7 Apply glue to the back of the bows and arrange them among the branches.

8 Prepare a decorative multi-loop bow and glue it to the top of the tree.

ORANGE TOPIARY TRE

A medley of orange-and-white eggs and green bows adorn this delightful little tree.

WHAT YOU'LL NEED

- 20–24 quail eggs
- Orange varnish
- Paintbrush
- Orange and white waxes
- Paraffin stove
- Pin stylus
- Fabric glue
- Green satin ribbon 1/2"
(12 mm) wide
- Scissors, measuring tape
- Artificial topiary tree with
6" (15 cm) diameter ball

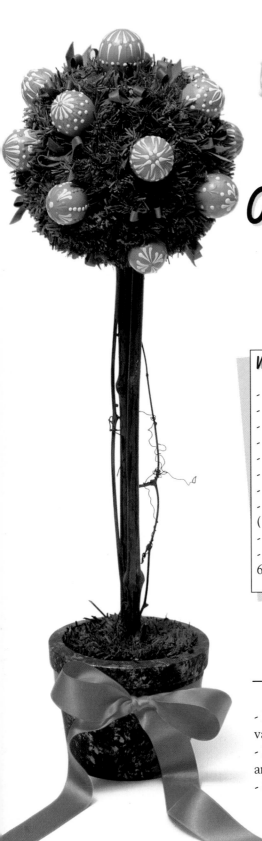

HOW TO'S

- Paint the eggs with orange varnish.
- Emboss the eggs with white and orange waxes.
- Seal the blowholes; see step 6

on page 21. Glue the eggs to the tree.
- Use the green ribbon to prepare 20–24 bows. Glue them to the tree.

DRILLING

The illusion of delicately embroidered eyelet lace is created by embossing snow-white eggs with white wax and drilling out the eyelets.

THE BASICS

- The uniqueness and beauty of drilled eggs comes from both the embossing and the holes.
- For drilled eggs, be sure to plan the designs on paper first.
- Using a measuring tape and pencil, measure and mark the locations on the shell where you wish to drill the holes.
- Make the holes with the power drill, which comes with different sizes and shapes of bits for making holes of all sizes quickly and accurately.
- Test the smaller drill bits on various test eggs, then use whichever bits give you the most satisfactory results.
- Remember that the stability and sturdiness of the shell will decrease as the number of holes increases.

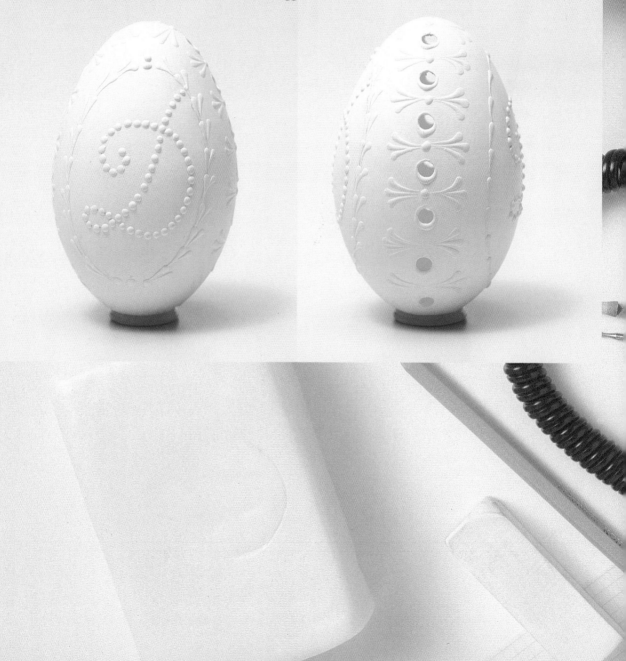

LACED EGGS

Drilled eggs laced prettily with narrow ribbons are an unusual surprise
to find in an Easter basket.

WHAT YOU'LL NEED

- Chicken or duck eggs
- Hard pencil
- Power drill or round file,
  assorted small bits
- Satin ribbons 1/8" (5 mm) wide
- Scissors, measuring tape
- Curved upholstery needle
- Small brush, soap
- Curtain rings

1 First draw on paper the patterns you wish to create on the eggs.

2 Use a pencil to mark 12 equal-sized segments around one egg.

3 About 3/4" (2 cm) from each blowhole, draw a circle around the end of the egg. Darken the points where the circles intersect the segment lines; these will be the locations of the large drilled holes.

4 Draw another circle around the middle of the egg, creating another 12 intersection points; darken 3 of them, making sure they are equidistant from each other; these points will also become large holes.

5 Drill out the large holes, making them all the same diameter.

6 At the ends of the egg, mark 3 small holes in the shape of a triangle centered above each group of 3 large holes, as shown.

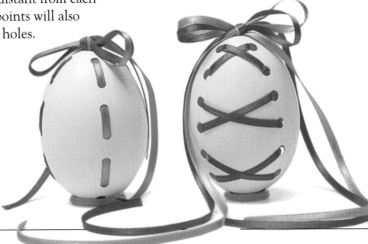

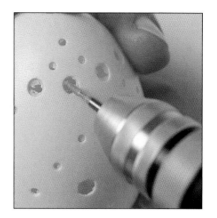

7 Draw a diamond around each one of the 3 holes around the center of the egg, marking 3 dots along each side of the diamond. You should have 8 dots forming each diamond.

8 Using a smaller drill bit than for the large holes, make a small hole at each dot on the triangles and diamonds.

9 Smooth the edges of all the holes, using the drill or round file.

10 After drilling the egg, use the small brush and soap to wash it thoroughly but carefully. Allow to dry.

11 Use the pencil to divide the egg into 4 equal top-to-bottom segments, then decorate each segment with wax as desired.
12 Drill 7 equidistant holes along each of the 4 pencil lines.
13 Thread the ribbon into the curved needle, then lace the egg.

14 Tie the ribbon end at the top of the egg.
15 Display the egg on a curtain-ring base.

PARTY FAVORS

Charmingly unique, these eyelet party favors make a special event even more special.

These favors are glued to small wooden curtain rings that have been coated with white varnish and then covered with fancy trims.

WHAT YOU'LL NEED

- White wax
- Paraffin stove
- Pin stylus
- Goose or chicken egg
- Hard pencil
- Power drill, assorted small bits
- Round file
- Small brush, soap

1 Use a pencil to mark a row of 7 equidistant dots along one side of the egg between the two blowholes.

2 Drill a hole at each marked dot, making all the holes the same size and centered around the dots.

3 Smooth the edges of the holes, using the drill or round file.

4 Melt some white wax and use it to draw around each hole, making 2 strokes of wax to complete each ring; the strokes can be drawn in the same or opposite directions, as long as they form a smooth, unbroken lip around the hole.

5 Hold the egg horizontally and make the center vertical stroke of a fleur-de-lis about 3/8" (1 cm) long between pairs of holes. Draw the strokes from the top downward.

6 Complete each fleur-de-lis by adding the shorter side strokes.

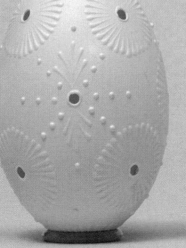

7 Rotate the egg 180 degrees and draw fleur-de-lis flowers on the opposite side of the holes; always draw the center petal first and then the outer ones.

8 Add a drop of wax between holes so that the dots are centered between the holes and flowers.

9 If you wish to personalize the egg, add one or two initials of the person to whom you want to give the egg. Mark the letters in pencil before embossing them.

10 Working along the pencil outline of the letter, make wax dots spaced very closely but not touching.

11 Draw an oval frame around the letter, making as many individual strokes as it takes.

12 Wash the egg with the small brush and soap in order to eliminate any remaining pencil marks.

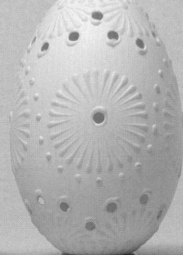

PLACE CARDS

These drilled and initialed eggs can be used as place markers and then taken home as party favors.

HOW-TO'S

- Paint the eggs gold if you plan to use them at a Christmas dinner, or paint them with colors that coordinate with your tablecloth and plates.
- These eggs were drilled, painted gold, then embossed with blue wax.
- Remember to always pierce the egg before you begin to color it.
- Emboss the letters using the dotted-line method; see step 10 on page 87.
- To make the bases, glue flowers and fancy trims around curtain rings.

WHAT YOU'LL NEED

- Large chicken eggs, pierced
- Gold paint
- Paintbrush
- Wooden skewers
- Blue wax
- Paraffin stove
- Pin stylus
- Curtain rings
- Blue and gold silk flowers
- White glue

BLUE-AND-PINK MOBILE

Dainty-looking drilled and painted eggs suspended between ribbons and bows lend a touch of whimsy to this imaginative mobile.

WHAT YOU'LL NEED

- 5 large, 4 medium, and 4 small chicken eggs
- Hard pencil
- Power drill, assorted small bits
- Light blue and pink varnishes
- Paintbrushes
- Wooden skewers
- Paraffin stove
- Pin stylus
- Round metal ring or hoop 8"–9" (22.5–23 cm) wide
- Fabric glue
- Picot-edged light blue satin ribbon 3/16" (0.5 cm) wide
- Turquoise satin ribbon 3/8" (1 cm) wide
- Light blue thread
- Sewing needle, scissors
- Measuring tape, curtain rings
- Long, straight upholstery needle

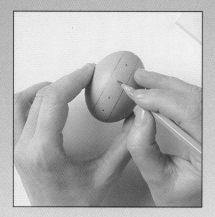

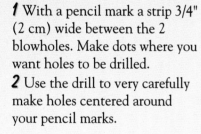

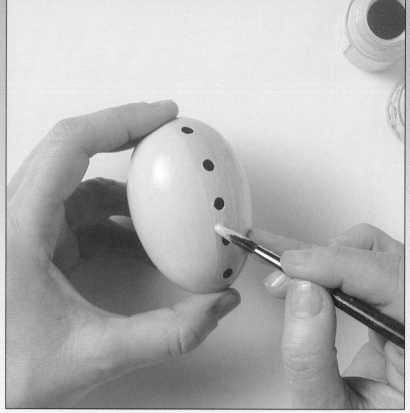

1 With a pencil mark a strip 3/4" (2 cm) wide between the 2 blowholes. Make dots where you want holes to be drilled.

2 Use the drill to very carefully make holes centered around your pencil marks.

3 Paint the sides of the egg (not the strip) with light blue varnish. Allow to dry.

4 Paint the strip with pink varnish.

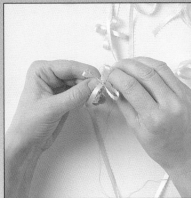

5 Paint the desired patterns and motifs on the sides and strip, using the light blue and pink waxes.
- If you wish, emboss an initial on one or both sides of the egg.

6 Cut 4 pieces of light blue ribbon, each 55" (140 cm) long.
7 At one end of each ribbon, make a 4-loop bow.
8 Use the upholstery needle to thread the free end of the ribbon through each of 4 large eggs.

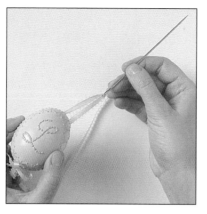

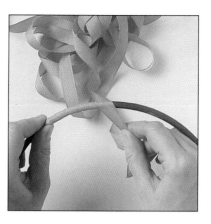

9 Leave about 3" (7.5 cm) of the ribbon extending above the egg, then tie another 4-loop bow; thread the free end of the ribbon through the medium-size eggs.

10 Repeat step 9 using the small eggs.

11 Prepare the center strand: Cut a piece of ribbon 5' (150 cm) long. Make a 4-loop bow at one end of the ribbon, then thread the opposite end through the egg on which you have embossed the initials.

12 Cover the round metal ring by wrapping the turquoise ribbon around it; glue it in place.

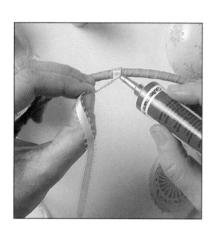

13 Cut 2 pieces of light blue ribbon about 24" (60 cm) long and thread them through a curtain ring that will be the hanger.

14 Sew or glue the ribbons and 4 long strands of eggs to the ring to complete the mobile.

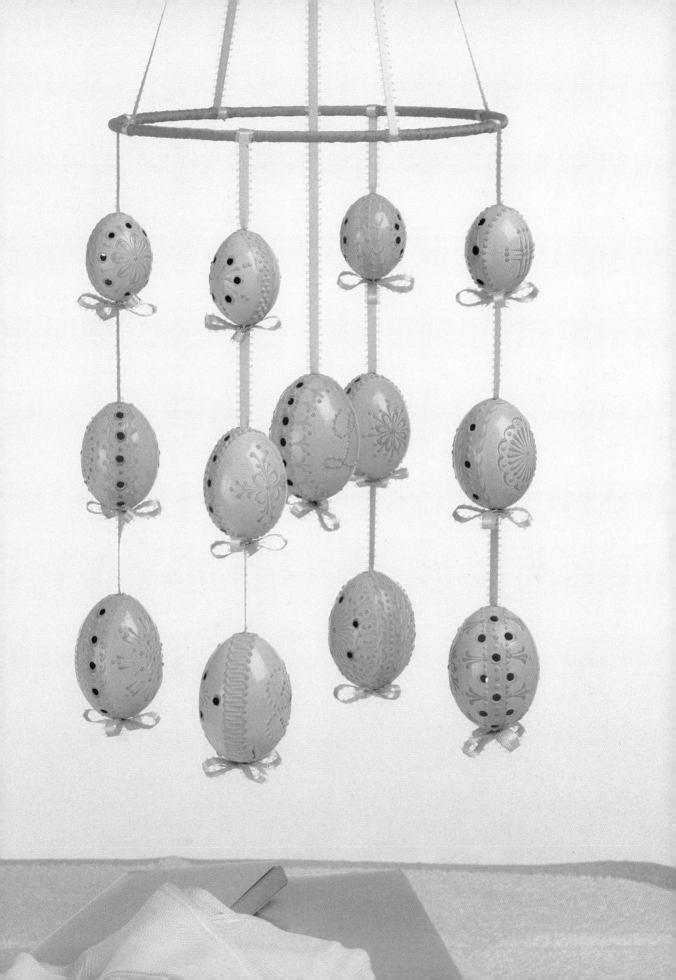

EASTER BASKET

Here's an idea for an unusual gift: drilled eggs laced with colorful ribbons.

HOW-TO'S

First sketch on paper the pattern you want to create on the egg, and then drill the holes.
- Varnish the eggs, allowing them to dry thoroughly after each coat.
- Thread ribbons through the holes, using the curved needle. Tie the ribbon ends into bows.
- Fill the straw basket with the laced eggs.

WHAT YOU'LL NEED

- Chicken eggs
- Wooden skewers
- Yellow and green varnishes, 3 shades of each.
- Curved upholstery needle
- Yellow and green satin ribbons about 1/8" (4 mm) wide, 3 shades of each
- Power drill, assorted small bits
- Straw basket

WAX RESIST

Wax resist is a typically Ukrainian technique of egg decorating. You can draw simple but elegant geometrics on a three-tone egg or experiment with more elaborate designs.

THE BASICS

- Similar to the batik wax-resist method of dying fabric, this egg-decorating technique involves painting with melted wax the parts of the egg intended to remain undyed.
- Beeswax is used because it is soft and easily removed after the coloring is completed.
- A wide range of fabric dyes is available. Use those recommended for batik, but never use the fixative that comes with the dye.
- Wax can be applied with the pin stylus.

SHINY BLACK EGGS

Soft daisies applied in this simple yet impressive technique give eggs a look of oriental charm.

WHAT YOU'LL NEED

- Goose egg
- Beeswax
- Paraffin stove
- Pin stylus
- Red fabric dye
- Rubber gloves
- Soft kitchen towels
- India ink
- Paintbrush

HOW-TO'S

1 Wash the egg in warm water, omitting vinegar because it would prevent the color from being properly absorbed.
2 Melt the beeswax. You can use flakes or pellets of white wax or sheets of yellow wax; the latter is softer and easier to remove.

3 Around the 2 blowholes on the egg, draw 8 equidistant wax rays about 1/2" (1.5 cm) long. If you prefer, you can mark off the egg into fourths or eighths before beginning to apply the wax.

4 Paint a deep scallop around each ray, creating the contiguous petals of a daisy.
5 Paint similar daisies in 2 or 4 of the marked egg segments, then complete the decorating as you wish.

6 Close the blowholes with a couple of drops of wax. This is extremely important because sealing the ends will prevent dye from getting inside the egg during dying.

7 Prepare the dye according to the manufacturer's directions.

8 Dip the egg into the dye, making sure the temperature does not exceed 104–113° F (40–45° C). Higher temperatures will melt the wax. - Keep the egg immersed in the dye for about 15 minutes, turning it constantly to get even coverage. Remember that the result of dying will depend on the intensity of the color, the duration of the immersion, and the temperature of the dip.

9 Remove the egg from the dye and delicately pat it dry with a clean towel.

10 Quickly and carefully pass the egg over a flame in order to melt the beeswax.

11 With a clean towel, carefully remove the wax; the beautiful white of the natural shell will appear through the red.

12 On this page and the one opposite, you will find variations to steps 1–11. Emboss the egg with daisies, dip it into the dye; dry it well; then add wax strokes and dots among the petals at both ends of the egg.

13 Decorate the sides of the egg as you desire.

14 Use a paintbrush to cover the egg completely with India ink.

15 Allow the ink to dry for 30 minutes and then with a clean towel remove any excess ink.

16 Carefully pass the egg over a flame to melt the wax.

17 Using another clean towel, remove the melted wax; the design will gradually appear.

- Remember when doing multiple dips to start with the lightest color and proceed in order toward the darkest.

PACKAGE TRIMS

Gift boxes look too pretty to open when they are dressed up with
wax-resist eggs, branches, and dried flowers.

- Blow and wash the egg in water only (no vinegar); clean it thoroughly with a scouring sponge.
- Melt the beeswax and use it to paint the egg as you wish.

- Dip the egg into the dye and then pat it dry.
- Pass the egg over a flame to melt the wax; remove the wax with a clean towel.

- You can dye your eggs to complement or contrast with the gift wrap, paper, ribbon, and other trims.

WHAT YOU'LL NEED

- Quail eggs
- Scouring sponge
- Beeswax, fabric dye
- Paraffin stove
- Pin stylus
- Soft towel

EASTER TREE

WHAT YOU'LL NEED

- Chicken or goose eggs
- Fabric dye
- Beeswax
- Paraffin stove
- Pin stylus
- Soft towel
- Long, straight upholstery needle
- Paintbrush
- Assorted ribbons
- Tree branch

HOW-TO'S

- Wash and blow the eggs.
- Melt some beeswax and use it to paint the eggs.
- Prepare fabric dye according to the manufacturer's directions and immerse the eggs, turning them constantly.
- Remove the eggs from the dye. Allow them to drip a little and then dry.

- Carefully pass the eggs over the flame in order to melt the wax; remove the wax with a clean towel.
- Use the upholstery needle to thread the colored ribbons through the blowholes; knot the ends.
- Hang the eggs on a branch.

DECOUPAGE

Decoupage is a decorating technique that involves no drawing or painting. It consists of cutting out and gluing onto the egg paper images, motifs, and shapes from newspapers, books, or magazines.

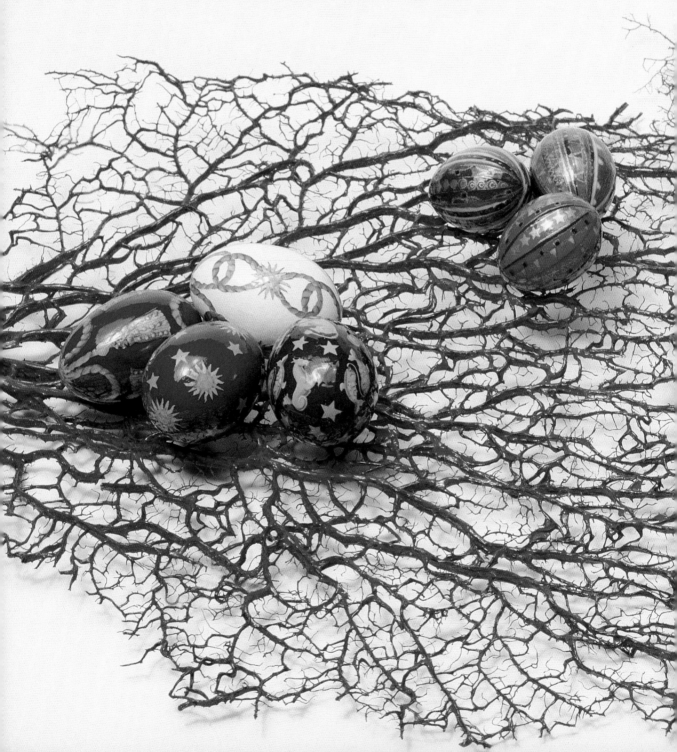

THE BASICS

- Traditional decoupage is a technique in which paper cutouts are glued onto a smooth surface.
- You can find decorative motifs in magazines, newspapers, albums, and decoupage books.
- Use a small pair of curved decoupage scissors to cut out your paper shapes.
- The cutouts are generally glued onto the egg with a slightly diluted decoupage glue that is similar to regular all-purpose white glue. It is also possible to use a nonpermanent spray fixative.
- Finish the eggs with one or more coats of transparent glossy, or satin, varnishes. Remember that if you use decoupage glue as the finishing, you must give the egg several coats to make sure the surface is smooth. Also note that decoupage glue may turn yellow over time.
- Smooth and durable finishes can be achieved with polyurethane paints, which are easy to use and give good results even after just one coat.
- You can also decoupage with pressed flowers and leaves, fabrics, stamps, and greeting cards.

STRIP PIECING

WHAT YOU'LL NEED

- Chicken eggs
- Gift wrap paper
- Decoupage glue, clear polyurethane paint
- Paintbrushes
- Decoupage scissors

1 Cut out a number of paper strips 1/8"–1/4" (3–6 mm) wide and slightly longer than the egg.

2 Use a paintbrush to spread decoupage glue over the back of the strips.

3 Wrap the first strip around the egg from top to bottom; glue an identical strip around the opposite side of the egg.
- If you will cover one or more blowholes of the egg with a bow, you can omit covering the holes with paper.

4 Glue on additional strips, butting or overlapping them so that none of the shell shows through.

5 Allow the egg to dry thoroughly at least 24 hours, then finish it with several thin coats of decoupage glue or polyurethane paint. Remember to allow the egg to dry thoroughly after each coat.

DECALS

WHAT YOU'LL NEED

- Chicken eggs
- Colored varnish
- Paintbrushes, scissors
- Gift wrap paper
- Nonpermanent spray fixative
- Decoupage glue

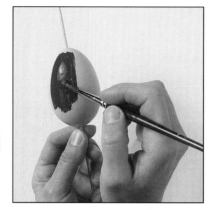

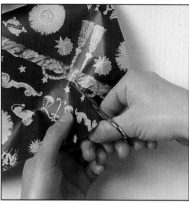

1 Paint a blown and washed egg with the colored varnish. Give it 2–3 thin coats and allow to dry thoroughly after each coat.

2 For this egg we cut out tassel, cord, and star motifs from gift wrap paper.

3 Spray the back of the cutouts with fixative and position them on the egg. The fixative is nonpermanent, which means you can reposition cutouts until you are satisfied.

4 Cover the blowhole at the base of the egg by gluing a small decal over it.

5 Finish the shell with several coats of decoupage glue.

FLORALS

Festive flowers can be given as gifts or they can hang on your own front door as pretty good-luck charms all year round.

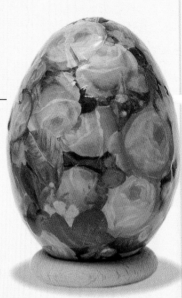

HOW-TO'S

- Cut out small flower motifs from gift wrap paper.
- Glue the cutouts all over the egg. Allow to dry.
- When the egg is completely dry, give it enough coats of decoupage glue to make the shell smooth.

- Glue ribbon to the top blowhole of the egg. Add a ribbon bow, if desired.
- Hang the egg from a bouquet of flowers.

WHAT YOU'LL NEED

- Chicken eggs
- Gift wrap paper with floral motifs
- Decoupage scissors
- Paintbrushes
- Decoupage glue
- Narrow satin ribbon
- White glue
- Fresh or dried flowers

GOLD-AND-RED GARLAND

This golden garland is an attractive and elegant
Christmas decoration suitable for hanging over the door,
on the Christmas tree, or on the wall.

WHAT YOU'LL NEED

- Chicken eggs
- Red-and-black plaid paper
- Scissors
- Decoupage glue
- Clear polyurethane paint
- Paintbrushes
- Red velvet ribbon
- Garland of naturals

HOW-TO'S

- Cut out a few strips of paper and glue them vertically onto the egg using decoupage glue.
- Allow to dry, then finish the egg with several thin coats of clear polyurethane paint.
- Glue the ribbon over the top blowhole of the egg, and tie it into a bow on the garland.
- You can make your own garland with dried fruit and ribbon bows sprayed with gold paint.

CHRISTMAS ORNAMENTS

Here are lots of eggs decorated with the decoupage method. Make yours bright and shiny for the holidays!

HOW-TO'S

- Cut out a number of paper strips 1/8"–1/4" (3–6 mm) wide and slightly longer than the egg.
- Spread decoupage glue on the back of the strips and press them onto the egg one at a time. Allow to dry.

- Finish the egg with a coat or two of clear polyurethane.
- Tie red bows, then glue one to each egg and hang the egg on a tree branch. Complete the tree with white-and-gold bows distributed evenly all over the tree.

STICKERS GALORE

This oh-so-simple egg-decorating technique
appeals to the child in all of us.

— HOW-TO'S —

- Wash and blow the eggs, then
paint them with colored
varnish.
- Glue small stickers all over the
egg; create simple but eye-
catching arrangements.
- Complete each egg by giving it
2–3 thin coats of clear acrylic
spray.

WHAT YOU'LL NEED

- Goose, chicken, and dove eggs
- Assorted colored varnishes
- Paintbrushes
- Small adhesive-backed stickers
- Clear acrylic spray

TRICKS OF THE TRADE

WASHING AWAY STAINS

Eggs – particularly those from geese – are frequently so dirty that hot water and soap are just not strong enough to clean them. If stains or yellow marks persist, use a scouring pad and liquid detergent.

POSITIONING BLOWHOLES

It isn't difficult to mark blowholes that are perfectly equidistant all around: Mark the centers of the two ends with a pencil, then check with a measuring tape in at least three different locations and adjust as necessary.

MAKING PERFECT BLOWHOLES

To make perfect blowholes, use a small drill to make the holes instead of a tapestry needle.

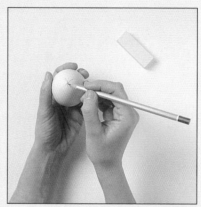

THICK OR THIN STROKES?

Wax-embossing strokes may be either thick or thin. The thickness depends on the temperature of the wax, the size of the pinhead, and the length of the pin. It especially depends on the amount of wax: If there is just a little wax, the stroke will come out thin. If there is a lot of wax, it will be thick and dense.

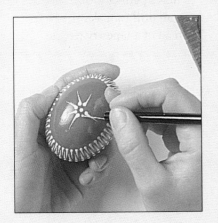

WHAT IF THE WAX OVERHEATS?

When the flame is too high, wax will overheat, start to smoke, produce noxious fumes, and change color. Overheated white wax turns yellow; other colored waxes turn gray. To prevent overheating you can remove the paraffin bottle from the stove for a few minutes to allow the wax to cool down, then put back the bottle and continue working.

WHAT IF I MAKE A MISTAKE?

If you are not completely satisfied with any of your wax embossing, carefully pass the egg over a flame and wipe away the wax with a clean cloth as it melts.

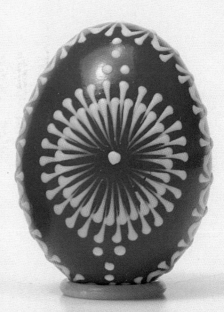

HANGING AN EGG

The easiest way to hang an egg is to bend a piece of wire about 12" (30 cm) long in half, twist it, and then thread it through the two blowholes after having inserted it into the looped end of the cord for hanging the egg.

BLEACHING QUAIL EGGS

Soaking quail eggs in a solution of water and vinegar for 15 minutes will get rid of the patina on the shells and leave them white or cream color.

MAKING SMOOTH ENDS

To prevent a buildup of overlapping layers of paper around the blowholes, just taper off the ends of each strip and poke them into the holes with the aid of a toothpick.

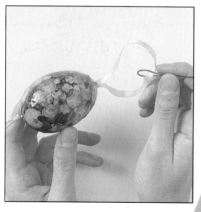

INDEX